Chimpanzees

by Helen Frost

Consulting Editor: Gail Saunders-Smith, Ph.D.

Consultants: Craig Stanford, Ph.D.,
Professor and Chair, Department of Anthropology,
University of Southern California

Pebble Books

an imprint of Capstone Press
Mankato, Minnesota

Pebble Books are published by Capstone Press
151 Good Counsel Drive, P.O. Box 669, Mankato, Minnesota 56002
http://www.capstone-press.com

Library of Congress Cataloging-in-Publication Data
Frost, Helen, 1949–
    Chimpanzees / by Helen Frost.
    p. cm.—(Rain forest animals)
    Summary: Simple text and photographs present the features and behavior
of chimpanzees.
    Includes bibliographical references (p. 23) and index.
    ISBN 0-7368-1455-8 (hardcover)
    1. Chimpanzees—Juvenile literature. [1. Chimpanzees. 2. Rain forest animals.]
I. Title. II. Series.
QL737.P96 F759 2003
599.885—dc21   2002001228

Note to Parents and Teachers

The Rain Forest Animals series supports national science standards related to life science. This book describes and illustrates chimpanzees that live in tropical rain forests. The photographs support early readers in understanding the text. The repetition of words and phrases helps early readers learn new words. This book also introduces early readers to subject-specific vocabulary words, which are defined in the Words to Know section. Early readers may need assistance to read some words and to use the Table of Contents, Words to Know, Read More, Internet Sites, and Index/Word List sections of the book.

Table of Contents

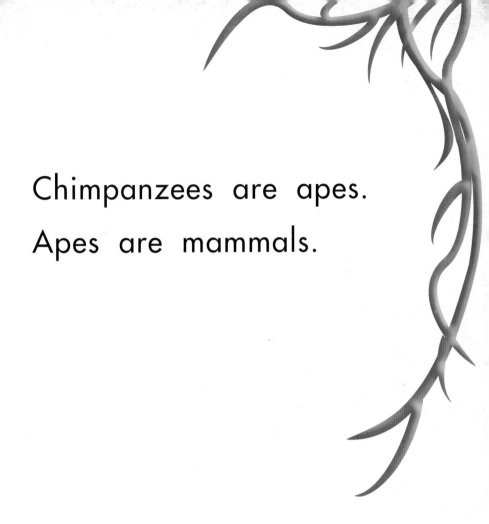

Chimpanzees are apes.

Apes are mammals.

Chimpanzees have long black fur.
They groom each other.

places chimpanzees live

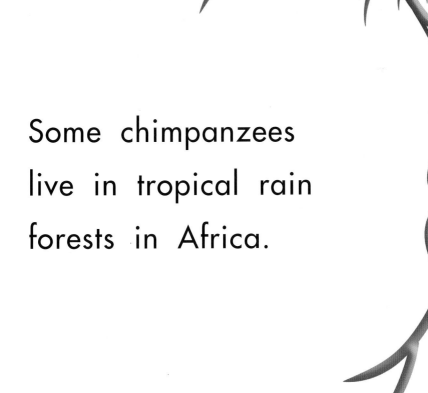

Some chimpanzees live in tropical rain forests in Africa.

emergent layer

canopy layer

understory layer

forest floor

Chimpanzees walk
along the forest floor.
They hang from trees
in the canopy layer.

Chimpanzees live
in groups.

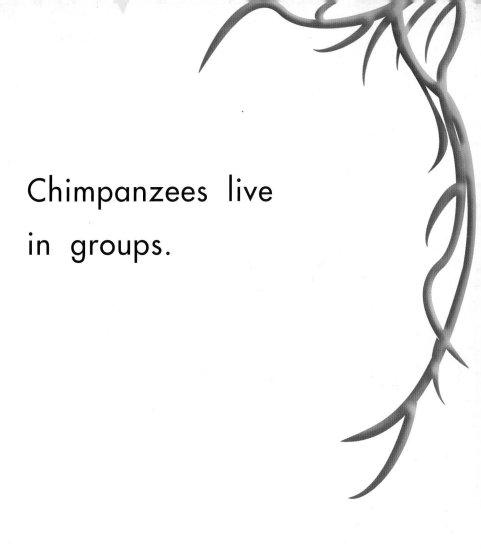

Chimpanzees travel
and look for food
during the day.

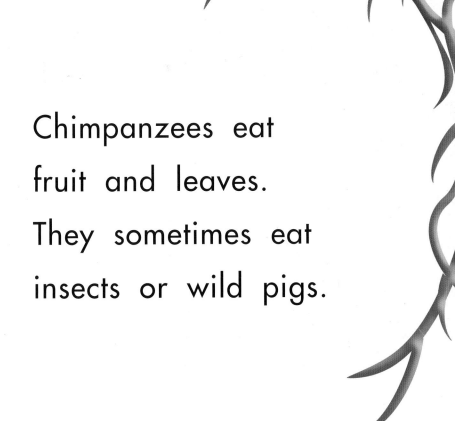

Chimpanzees eat
fruit and leaves.
They sometimes eat
insects or wild pigs.

18

Chimpanzees use sticks
and rocks as tools.
They pick up insects.
They open nuts.

a young chimpanzee learning how to
use a stick to pick up ants

Chimpanzees rest at night.
They make nests in trees.

Words to Know

ape—a large primate with no tail; gorillas, orangutans, and chimpanzees are kinds of apes.

canopy—the layer of treetops that forms a covering over a rain forest

forest floor—the bottom layer of a rain forest

groom—to clean; chimpanzees groom each other by picking bugs off each other's fur.

insect—a small animal with a hard outer shell, six legs, and wings

mammal—a warm-blooded animal with a backbone; female mammals feed milk to their young.

nest—a cozy place or shelter; chimpanzees use branches and leaves to build nests in trees.

tool—something used to make work easier

tropical rain forest—a thick area of trees in a warm place where rain falls almost every day

Read More

Donovan, Sandra. *Chimpanzees.* Animals of the Rain Forest. Austin, Texas: Raintree Steck-Vaughn, 2002.

Greenberg, Daniel. *Chimpanzees.* Animals, Animals. New York: Marshall Cavendish, 2001.

Kendell, Patricia. *Chimpanzees.* In the Wild. Austin, Texas: Raintree Steck-Vaughn, 2002.

Internet Sites

All about Chimpanzees
http://www.enchantedlearning.com/subjects/apes/chimp

Chimpanzee Vocalizations
http://www.emory.edu/LIVING_LINKS/a/vocalizations.html

The Jane Goodall Institute: Chimpanzees
http://www.janegoodall.org/chimps

World Wide Fund for Nature: Chimpanzee
http://www.panda.org/kids/wildlife/mnchimp.htm

Index/Word List

Word Count: 86
Early-Intervention Level: 12

Editorial Credits

Martha E. H. Rustad, editor; Linda Clavel and Heidi Meyer, cover designers; Jennifer Schonborn, interior illustrator; Angi Gahler, book designer; Wanda Winch, photo researcher; Karen Risch, product planning editor

Photo Credits

Aurora/Michael Nichols, 12
Bruce Coleman Inc./Helmut Albrecht, 14
Corbis/Kennan Ward, cover, 20
DigitalVision, 8
McDonald Wildlife Photography/Joe McDonald, 16
Minden Pictures/Gerry Ellis, 6, 18 (both)
PhotoDisc, Inc., 1
Photo Network/Mark Newman, 4

The author thanks the children's section staff at the Allen County Public Library in Fort Wayne, Indiana, for research assistance.